The Poetry Of Herman Melville, Volume 1

Index Of Poems

America

I

Where the wings of a sunny Dome expand

I saw a Banner in gladsome air

Starry, like Berenice's Hair

Afloat in broadened bravery there;

With undulating long-drawn flow,

As rolled Brazilian billows go

Voluminously o'er the Line.

The Land reposed in peace below;

The children in their glee

Were folded to the exulting heart

Of young Maternity.

II

Later, and it streamed in fight

When tempest mingled with the fray,

And over the spear-point of the shaft

I saw the ambiguous lightning play.

Valor with Valor strove, and died:
Fierce was Despair, and cruel was Pride;
And the lorn Mother speechless stood,
Pale at the fury of her brood.

III
Yet later, and the silk did wind
Her fair cold for;
Little availed the shining shroud,
Though ruddy in hue, to cheer or warm
A watcher looked upon her low, and said
She sleeps, but sleeps, she is not dead.
But in that sleep contortion showed
The terror of the vision there
A silent vision unavowed,
Revealing earth's foundation bare,
And Gorgon in her hidden place.
It was a thing of fear to see
So foul a dream upon so fair a face,
And the dreamer lying in that starry shroud.

IV
But from the trance she sudden broke
The trance, or death into promoted life;
At her feet a shivered yoke,
And in her aspect turned to heaven
No trace of passion or of strife
A clear calm look. It spake of pain,
But such as purifies from stain
Sharp pangs that never come again
And triumph repressed by knowledge meet,
Power delicate, and hope grown wise,
And youth matured for age's seat
Law on her brow and empire in her eyes.
So she, with graver air and lifted flag;
While the shadow, chased by light,
Fled along the far-brawn height,
And left her on the crag.

Formerly A Slave
The sufferance of her race is shown,
And retrospect of life,
Which now too late deliverance dawns upon;
Yet is she not at strife.

Her children's children they shall know
The good withheld from her;
And so her reverie takes prophetic cheer
In spirit she sees the stir.

Far down the depth of thousand years,
And marks the revel shine;
Her dusky face is lit with sober light,
Sibylline, yet benign.

Crossing The Tropics

From 'The Saya-y-Manto.'

While now the Pole Star sinks from sight
The Southern Cross it climbs the sky;
But losing thee, my love, my light,
O bride but for one bridal night,
The loss no rising joys supply.

Love, love, the Trade Winds urge abaft,
And thee, from thee, they steadfast waft.

By day the blue and silver sea
And chime of waters blandly fanned
Nor these, nor Gama's stars to me
May yield delight since still for thee
I long as Gama longed for land.

I yearn, I yearn, reverting turn,
My heart it streams in wake astern
When, cut by slanting sleet, we swoop
Where raves the world's inverted year,
If roses all your porch shall loop,
Not less your heart for me will droop
Doubling the world's last outpost drear.

O love, O love, these oceans vast:
Love, love, it is as death were past!

Art

In placid hours well-pleased we dream
Of many a brave unbodied scheme.
But form to lend, pulsed life create,
What unlike things must meet and mate:
A flame to melt, a wind to freeze;
Sad patience, joyous energies;
Humility, yet pride and scorn;
Instinct and study; love and hate;
Audacity, reverence. These must mate,
And fuse with Jacob's mystic heart,
To wrestle with the angel, Art.

A Utilitarian View Of The Monitor's Fight

Plain be the phrase, yet apt the verse,
More ponderous than nimble;
For since grimed War here laid aside
His painted pomp, 'twould ill befit
Overmuch to ply
The rhyme's barbaric symbol.

Hail to victory without the gaud
Of glory; zeal that needs no fans
Of banners; plain mechanic power
Plied cogently in War now placed
Where War belongs
Among the trades and artisans.

Yet this was battle, and intense
Beyond the strife of fleets heroic;
Deadlier, closer, calm 'mid storm;
No passion; all went on by crank.
Pivot, and screw,
And calculations of caloric.

Needless to dwell; the story's known.
The ringing of those plates on plates
Still ringeth round the world
The clangor of the blacksmiths' fray.
The anvil-din
Resounds this message from the Fates:

War shall yet be, and to the end;
But war-paint shows the streaks of weather;
War yet shall be, but the warriors
Are now but operatives; War's made
Less grand than Peace,
And a singe runs through lace and feather.

An Uninscribed Monument on One of the Battle-Fields of the Wilderness

Silence and solitude may hint
(Whose home is in yon piney wood)
What I, though tableted, could never tell
The din which here befell,
And striving of the multitude.
The iron cones and spheres of death
Set round me in their rust,
These, too, if just,
Shall speak with more than animated breath.
Thou who beholdest, if thy thought,
Not narrowed down to personal cheer,
Take in the import of the quiet here
The after-quiet, the calm full fraught;
Thou too wilt silent stand

Silent as I, and lonesome as the land.

Ball's Bluff : A Reverie

One noonday, at my window in the town,
I saw a sight - saddest that eyes can see
Young soldiers marching lustily
Unto the wars,
With fifes, and flags in mottoed pageantry;
While all the porches, walks, and doors
Were rich with ladies cheering royally.

They moved like Juny morning on the wave,
Their hearts were fresh as clover in its prime
(It was the breezy summer time),
Life throbbed so strong,
How should they dream that Death in rosy clime
Would come to thin their shining throng?
Youth feels immortal, like the gods sublime.

Weeks passed; and at my window, leaving bed,
By nights I mused, of easeful sleep bereft,
On those brave boys (Ah War! thy theft);
Some marching feet
Found pause at last by cliffs Potomac cleft;
Wakeful I mused, while in the street
Far footfalls died away till none were left.

A Bridegroom Dick

1876

Sunning ourselves in October on a day
Balmy as spring, though the year was in decay,
I lading my pipe, she stirring her tea,
My old woman she says to me,
'Feel ye, old man, how the season mellows?'
And why should I not, blessed heart alive,
Here mellowing myself, past sixty-five,
To think o' the May-time o' pennoned young
fellows
This stripped old hulk here for years may
survive.

Ere yet, long ago, we were spliced, Bonny Blue,
(Silvery it gleams down the moon-glade o' time,
Ah, sugar in the bowl and berries in the prime!)
Coxswain I o' the Commodore's crew,
Under me the fellows that manned his fine gig,
Spinning him ashore, a king in full fig.
Chirrupy even when crosses rubbed me,

Bridegroom Dick lieutenants dubbed me.
Pleasant at a yarn, Bob o' Linkum in a song,
Diligent in duty and nattily arrayed,
Favored I was, wife, and fleeted right along;
And though but a tot for such a tall grade,
A high quartermaster at last I was made.

All this, old lassie, you have heard before,
But you listen again for the sake e'en o' me;
No babble stales o' the good times o' yore
To Joan, if Darby the babbler be.

Babbler? O' what? Addled brains, they
forget!
O quartermaster I; yes, the signals set,
Hoisted the ensign, mended it when frayed,
Polished up the binnacle, minded the helm,
And prompt every order blithely obeyed.
To me would the officers say a word cheery
Break through the starch o' the quarter-deck
realm;
His coxswain late, so the Commodore's pet.
Ay, and in night-watches long and weary,
Bored nigh to death with the navy etiquette,
Yearning, too, for fun, some younker, a cadet,
Dropping for time each vain bumptious trick,
Boy-like would unbend to Bridegroom Dick.
But a limit there was, a check, d' ye see:
Those fine young aristocrats knew their degree.

Well, stationed aft where their lordships
keep,
Seldom going forward excepting to sleep,
I, boozing now on by-gone years,
My betters recall along with my peers.
Recall them? Wife, but I see them plain:
Alive, alert, every man stirs again.
Ay, and again on the lee-side pacing,
My spy-glass carrying, a truncheon in show,
Turning at the taffrail, my footsteps retracing,
Proud in my duty, again methinks I go.
And Dave, Dainty Dave, I mark where he
stands,
Our trim sailing-master, to time the high-noon,
That thingumbob sextant perplexing eyes and
hands,
Squinting at the sun, or twigging o' the moon;
Then, touching his cap to Old Chock-a-Block
Commanding the quarter-deck, 'Sir, twelve
o'clock.'

Where sails he now, that trim sailing-master,
Slender, yes, as the ship's sky-s'l pole?
Dimly I mind me of some sad disaster
Dainty Dave was dropped from the navy-roll!
And ah, for old Lieutenant Chock-a-Block
Fast, wife, chock-fast to death's black dock!
Buffeted about the obstreperous ocean,
Fleeted his life, if lagged his promotion.
Little girl, they are all, all gone, I think,
Leaving Bridegroom Dick here with lids that
wink.

Where is Ap Catesby? The fights fought of
yore
Famed him, and laced him with epaulets, and
more.
But fame is a wake that after-wakes cross,
And the waters wallow all, and laugh
Where's the loss?
But John Bull's bullet in his shoulder bearing
Ballasted Ap in his long sea-faring.
The middies they ducked to the man who had
messed
With Decatur in the gun-room, or forward
pressed
Fighting beside Perry, Hull, Porter, and the
rest.

Humped veteran o' the Heart-o'-Oak war,
Moored long in haven where the old heroes are,
Never on you did the iron-clads jar!
Your open deck when the boarder assailed,
The frank old heroic hand-to-hand then availed.

But where's Guert Gan? Still heads he the van?
As before Vera-Cruz, when he dashed splashing
through
The blue rollers sunned, in his brave gold-and-
blue,
And, ere his cutter in keel took the strand,
Aloft waved his sword on the hostile land!
Went up the cheering, the quick chanticleering;
All hands vying, all colors flying:
'Cock-a-doodle-doo!' and 'Row, boys, row!'
'Hey, Starry Banner!' 'Hi, Santa Anna!'
Old Scott's young dash at Mexico.

Fine forces o' the land, fine forces o' the sea,
Fleet, army, and flotilla, tell, heart o' me,
Tell, if you can, whereaway now they be!

But ah, how to speak of the hurricane
unchained
The Union's strands parted in the hawser
over-strained;
Our flag blown to shreds, anchors gone
altogether
The dashed fleet o' States in Secession's foul
weather.

Lost in the smother o' that wide public stress,
In hearts, private hearts, what ties there were
snapped!
Tell, Hal, vouch, Will, o' the ward-room mess,
On you how the riving thunder-bolt clapped.
With a bead in your eye and beads in your glass,
And a grip o' the flipper, it was part and pass:
'Hal, must it be: Well, if come indeed the
shock,
To North or to South, let the victory cleave,
Vaunt it he may on his dung-hill the cock,
But Uncle Sam's eagle never crow will,
believe.'

Sentiment: ay, while suspended hung all,
Ere the guns against Sumter opened there
the ball,
And partners were taken, and the red dance
began,
War's red dance o' death! Well, we, to a man,
We sailors o' the North, wife, how could we
lag?
Strike with your kin, and you stick to the flag!
But to sailors o' the South that easy way was
barred.
To some, dame, believe (and I speak o' what I
know),
Wormwood the trial and the Uzzite's black
shard;
And the faithfuller the heart, the crueller the
throe.
Duty? It pulled with more than one string,
This way and that, and anyhow a sting.
The flag and your kin, how be true unto both?
If either plight ye keep, then ye break the other
troth.
But elect here they must, though the casuists
were out;
Decide, hurry up, and throttle every doubt.

Of all these thrills thrilled at keelson, and
throes,

Little felt the shoddyites a-toasting o' their
toes;
In mart and bazar Lucre chuckled the huzza,
Coining the dollars in the bloody mint of war.

But in men, gray knights o' the Order o' Scars,
And brave boys bound by vows unto Mars,
Nature grappled honor, intertwisting in the
strife:
But some cut the knot with a thoroughgoing
knife.
For how when the drums beat? How in the fray
In Hampton Roads on the fine balmy day?

There a lull, wife, befell, drop o' silent in the
din.
Let us enter that silence ere the belchings
re-begin.
Through a ragged rift aslant in the cannonade's
smoke
An iron-clad reveals her repellent broadside
Bodily intact. But a frigate, all oak,
Shows honeycombed by shot, and her deck
crimson-dyed.
And a trumpet from port of the iron-clad hails,
Summoning the other, whose flag never trails:
'Surrender that frigate, Will! Surrender,
Or I will sink her ram, and end her!'

'T was Hal. And Will, from the naked heart-o'-oak,
Will, the old messmate, minus trumpet, spoke,
Informally intrepid, 'Sink her, and be
damned!'* [* Historic.]
Enough. Gathering way, the iron-clad rammed.
The frigate, heeling over, on the wave threw a
dusk.
Not sharing in the slant, the clapper of her bell
The fixed metal struck, uinvoked struck the
knell
Of the Cumberland stillettoed by the
Merrimac's tusk;
While, broken in the wound underneath the
gun-deck,
Like a sword-fish's blade in leviathan waylaid,
The tusk was left infixed in the fast-foundering
wreck.
There, dungeoned in the cockpit, the wounded
go down,
And the chaplain with them. But the surges
uplift
The prone dead from deck, and for moment

they drift
Washed with the swimmers, and the spent
swimmers drown.
Nine fathom did she sink, erect, though hid
from light
Save her colors unsurrendered and spars that
kept the height.

Nay, pardon, old aunty! Wife, never let it fall,
That big started tear that hovers on the brim;
I forgot about your nephew and the Merrimac's
ball;
No more then of her, since it summons up him.
But talk o' fellows' hearts in the wine's genial
cup:
Trap them in the fate, jam them in the strait,
Guns speak their hearts then, and speak
right up.
The troublous colic o' intestine war
It sets the bowels o' affection ajar.
But, lord, old dame, so spins the whizzing world,
A humming-top, ay, for the little boy-gods
Flogging it well with their smart little rods,
Tittering at time and the coil uncurled.

Now, now, sweetheart, you sidle away,
No, never you like that kind o' gay;
But sour if I get, giving truth her due,
Honey-sweet forever, wife, will Dick be to you!

But avast with the War! 'Why recall racking
days
Since set up anew are the slip's started stays?
Nor less, though the gale we have left behind,
Well may the heave o' the sea remind.
It irks me now, as it troubled me then,
To think o' the fate in the madness o' men.
If Dick was with Farragut on the night-river,
When the boom-chain we burst in the fire-raft's
glare,
That blood-dyed the visage as red as the liver;
In the Battle for the Bay too if Dick had a
share,
And saw one aloft a-piloting the war
Trumpet in the whirlwind, a Providence in
place
Our Admiral old whom the captains huzza,
Dick joys in the man nor brags about the race.

But better, wife, I like to booze on the days
Ere the Old Order foundered in these very

frays,
And tradition was lost and we learned strange
ways.
Often I think on the brave cruises then;
Re-sailing them in memory, I hail the press o'
men
On the gunned promenade where rolling they
go,
Ere the dog-watch expire and break up the
show.
The Laced Caps I see between forward guns;
Away from the powder-room they puff the
cigar;
'Three days more, hey, the donnas and the
dons!'
'Your Zeres widow, will you hunt her up,
Starr?'
The Laced Caps laugh, and the bright waves
too;
Very jolly, very wicked, both sea and crew,
Nor heaven looks sour on either, I guess,
Nor Pecksniff he bosses the gods' high mess.
Wistful ye peer, wife, concerned for my head,
And how best to get me betimes to my bed.

But king o' the club, the gayest golden spark,
Sailor o' sailors, what sailor do I mark?
Tom Tight, Tom Tight, no fine fellow finer,
A cutwater nose, ay, a spirited soul;
But, bowsing away at the well-brewed bowl,
He never bowled back from that last voyage to
China.

Tom was lieutenant in the brig-o'-war famed
When an officer was hung for an arch-mutineer,
But a mystery cleaved, and the captain was
blamed,
And a rumpus too raised, though his honor
it was clear.
And Tom he would say, when the mousers
would try him,
And with cup after cup o' Burgundy ply him:
'Gentlemen, in vain with your wassail you
beset,
For the more I tipple, the tighter do I get.'
No blabber, no, not even with the can
True to himself and loyal to his clan.

Tom blessed us starboard and damned us larboard,
Right down from rail to the streak o' the
garboard.

Nor less, wife, we liked him. Tom was a man
In contrast queer with Chaplain Le Fan,
Who blessed us at morn, and at night yet again,
Damning us only in decorous strain;
Preaching 'tween the guns, each cutlass in its
place
From text that averred old Adam a hard case.
I see him, Tom, on horse-block standing,
Trumpet at mouth, thrown up all amain,
An elephant's bugle, vociferous demanding
Of topmen aloft in the hurricane of rain,
'Letting that sail there your faces flog?
Manhandle it, men, and you'll get the good
grog!'
O Tom, but he knew a blue-jacket's ways,
And how a lieutenant may genially haze;
Only a sailor sailors heartily praise.

Wife, where be all these chaps, I wonder?
Trumpets in the tempest, terrors in the fray,
Boomed their commands along the deck like
thunder;
But silent is the sod, and thunder dies away.
But Captain Turret, 'Old Hemlock' tall,
(A leaning tower when his tank brimmed all,)
Manoeuvre out alive from the war did he?
Or, too old for that, drift under the lee?
Kentuckian colossal, who, touching at Madeira,
The huge puncheon shipped o' prime
Santa-Clara;
Then rocked along the deck so solemnly!
No whit the less though judicious was enough
In dealing with the Finn who made the great
huff;
Our three-decker's giant, a grand boatswain's
mate,
Manliest of men in his own natural senses;
But driven stark mad by the devil's drugged
stuff,
Storming all aboard from his run-ashore late,
Challenging to battle, vouchsafing no pretenses,
A reeling King Ogg, delirious in power,
The quarter-deck carronades he seemed to
make cower.
'Put him in brig there!' said Lieutenant
Marrot.
'Put him in brig!' back he mocked like a
parrot;
'Try it, then!' swaying a fist like Thor's
sledge,
And making the pigmy constables hedge

Ship's corporals and the master-at-arms.
'In brig there, I say!' They dally no more;
Like hounds let slip on a desperate boar,
Together they pounce on the formidable Finn,
Pinion and cripple and hustle him in.
Anon, under sentry, between twin guns,
He slides off in drowse, and the long night runs.

Morning brings a summons. Whistling it calls,
Shrilled through the pipes of the boatswain's
four aids;
Trilled down the hatchways along the dusk
halls:
Muster to the Scourge! Dawn of doom and
its blast!
As from cemeteries raised, sailors swarm before
the mast,
Tumbling up the ladders from the ship's nether
shades.

Keeping in the background and taking small
part,
Lounging at their ease, indifferent in face,
Behold the trim marines uncompromised in
heart;
Their Major, buttoned up, near the staff finds
Room
The staff o' lieutenants standing grouped in
their place.
All the Laced Caps o' the ward-room come,
The Chaplain among them, disciplined and
dumb.
The blue-nosed boatswain, complexioned like
slag,
Like a blue Monday lours, his implements in
bag.
Executioners, his aids, a couple by him stand,
At a nod there the thongs to receive from his hand.
Never venturing a caveat whatever may betide,
Though functionally here on humanity's side,
The grave Surgeon shows, like the formal
physician
Attending the rack o' the Spanish Inquisition.

The angel o' the 'brig' brings his prisoner up;
Then, steadied by his old Santa-Clara, a sup,
Heading all erect, the ranged assizes there,
Lo, Captain Turret, and under starred
bunting,
(A florid full face and fine silvered hair,)
Gigantic the yet greater giant confronting.

Now the culprit he liked, as a tall captain can
A Titan subordinate and true sailor-man;
And frequent he'd shown it, no worded
advance,
But flattering the Finn with a well-timed glance.
But what of that now? In the martinet-mien
Read the Articles of War, heed the naval
routine;
While, cut to the heart a dishonor there to win,
Restored to his senses, stood the Anak Finn;
In racked self-control the squeezed tears
peeping,
Scalding the eye with repressed inkeeping.
Discipline must be; the scourge is deemed due.
But ah for the sickening and strange heart-
benumbing,
Compassionate abasement in shipmates that view;
Such a grand champion shamed there succumbing!
'Brown, tie him up.' The cord he brooked:
How else? his arms spread apart, never
threaping;
No, never he flinched, never sideways he looked,
Peeled to the waistband, the marble flesh
creeping,
Lashed by the sleet the officious winds urge.

In function his fellows their fellowship merge,
The twain standing nigh, the two boatswain's
mates,
Sailors of his grade, ay, and brothers of his
mess.
With sharp thongs adroop the junior one
awaits
The word to uplift.
'Untie him so!
Submission is enough, Man, you may go.'
Then, promenading aft, brushing fat Purser
Smart,
'Flog? Never meant it, hadn't any heart.
Degrade that tall fellow? 'Such, wife, was he,
Old Captain Turret, who the brave wine could
stow.
Magnanimous, you think? But what does
Dick see?
Apron to your eye! Why, never fell a blow;
Cheer up, old wifie, 't was a long time ago.

But where's that sore one, crabbed and-severe,
Lieutenant Lon Lumbago, an arch scrutineer?
Call the roll to-day, would he answer Here!

When the Blixum's fellows to quarters
mustered
How he'd lurch along the lane of gun-crews
clustered,
Testy as touchwood, to pry and to peer.
Jerking his sword underneath larboard arm,
He ground his worn grinders to keep himself
calm.
Composed in his nerves, from the fidgets set
free,
Tell, Sweet Wrinkles, alive now is he,
In Paradise a parlor where the even
tempers be?

Where's Commander All-a-Tanto?
Where's Orlop Bob singing up from below?
Where's Rhyming Ned? has he spun his last
canto?
Where's Jewsharp Jim? Where's Ringadoon
Joe?
Ah, for the music over and done,
The band all dismissed save the droned
trombone!
Where's Glenn o' the gun-room, who loved
Hot-Scotch
Glen, prompt and cool in a perilous watch?
Where's flaxen-haired Phil? a gray lieutenant?
Or rubicund, flying a dignified pennant?

But where sleeps his brother? the cruise it was
o'er,
But ah, for death's grip that welcomed him
ashore!
Where's Sid, the cadet, so frank in his brag,
Whose toast was audacious'Here's Sid, and
Sid's flag!'
Like holiday-craft that have sunk unknown,
May a lark of a lad go lonely down?
Who takes the census under the sea?
Can others like old ensigns be,
Bunting I hoisted to flutter at the gaff
Rags in end that once were flags
Gallant streaming from the staff?

Such scurvy doom could the chances deal
To Top-Gallant Harry and Jack Genteel?
Lo, Genteel Jack in hurricane weather,
Shagged like a bear, like a red lion roaring;
But O, so fine in his chapeau and feather,
In port to the ladies never once jawing;
All bland politesse, how urbane was he

'Oui, mademoiselle' - 'Ma chere amie!'

'T was Jack got up the ball at Naples,
Gay in the old Ohio glorious;
His hair was curled by the berth-deck barber,
Never you'd deemed him a cub of rude Boreas;
In tight little pumps, with the grand dames in
rout,
A-flinging his shapely foot all about;
His watch-chain with love's jeweled tokens
abounding,
Curls ambrosial shaking out odors,
Waltzing along the batteries, astounding
The gunner glum and the grim-visaged loaders.

Wife, where be all these blades, I wonder,
Pennoned fine fellows, so strong, so gay?
Never their colors with a dip dived under;
Have they hauled them down in a lack-lustre
day,
Or beached their boats in the Far, Far Away?
Hither and thither, blown wide asunder,
Where's this fleet, I wonder and wonder.
Slipt their cables, rattled their adieu,
(Whereaway pointing? to what rendezvous?)
Out of sight, out of mind, like the crack
Constitution,
And many a keel time never shall renew
Bon Homme Dick o' the buff Revolution,
The Black Cockade and the staunch True-Blue.

Doff hats to Decatur! But where is his blazon?
Must merited fame endure time's wrong
Glory's ripe grape wizen up to a raisin?
Yes! for Nature teems, and the years are
strong,
And who can keep the tally o' the names that
fleet along!

But his frigate, wife, his bride? Would
blacksmiths brown
Into smithereens smite the solid old renown?
Rivetting the bolts in the iron-clad's shell,
Hark to the hammers with a rat-tat-tat;
'Handier a derby than a laced cocked hat!
The Monitor was ugly, but she served us right
well,
Better than the Cumberland, a beauty and the
belle.'

Better than the Cumberland! Heart alive

in me!
That battlemented hull, Tantallon o' the sea,
Kicked in, as at Boston the taxed chests o' tea!
Ay, spurned by the ram, once a tall, shapely
craft,
But lopped by the Rebs to an iron-beaked
raft
A blacksmith's unicorn in armor cap-a-pie.

Under the water-line a ram's blow is dealt:
And foul fall the knuckles that strike below the
belt.
Nor brave the inventions that serve to replace
The openness of valor while dismantling the
grace.

Aloof from all this and the never-ending game,
Tantamount to teetering, plot and counterplot;
Impenetrable armor, all-perforating shot;
Aloof, bless God, ride the war-ships of old,
A grand fleet moored in the roadstead of fame;
Not submarine sneaks with them are enrolled;
Their long shadows dwarf us, their flags are as
flame.

Don't fidget so, wife; an old man's passion
Amounts to no more than this smoke that I
puff;
There, there, now, buss me in good old fashion;
A died-down candle will flicker in the snuff.

But one last thing let your old babbler say,
What Decatur's coxswain said who was long
ago hearsed,
'Take in your flying-kites, for there comes a
lubber's day
When gallant things will go, and the three-
deckers first.'

My pipe is smoked out, and the grog runs
slack;
But bowse away, wife, at your blessed Bohea;
This empty can here must needs solace me
Nay, sweetheart, nay; I take that back;
Dick drinks from your eyes and he finds no
lack!

Dupont's Round Flight
In time and measure perfect moves
All Art whose aim is sure;

Evolving rhyme and stars divine
Have rules, and they endure.

Nor less the Fleet that warred for Right,
And, warring so, prevailed,
In geometric beauty curved,
And in an orbit sailed.

The rebel at Port Royal felt
The Unity overawe,
And rued the spell. A type was here,
And victory of LAW.

Epilogue

If Luther's day expand to Darwin's year,
Shall that exclude the hope, foreclose the fear?

Unmoved by all the claims our times avow,
The ancient Sphinx still keeps the porch of
shade;
And comes Despair, whom not her calm may
cow,
And coldly on that adamantine brow
Scrawls undeterred his bitter pasquinade.
But Faith (who from the scrawl indignant
turns)
With blood warm oozing from her wounded
trust,
Inscribes even on her shards of broken urns
The sign o' the cross, the spirit above the dust!

Yea, ape and angel, strife and old debate
The harps of heaven and dreary gongs of hell;
Science the feud can only aggravate
No umpire she betwixt the chimes and knell:
The running battle of the star and clod
Shall run forever, if there be no God.

Degrees we know, unknown in days before;
The light is greater, hence the shadow more;
And tantalized and apprehensive Man
Appealing, Wherefore ripen us to pain?
Seems there the spokesman of dumb Nature's
train.

But through such strange illusions have they
passed
Who in life's pilgrimage have baffled striven
Even death may prove unreal at the last,

And stoics be astounded into heaven.

Then keep thy heart, though yet but
ill-resigned
Clarel, thy heart, the issues there but mind;
That like the crocus budding through the
snow
That like a swimmer rising from the deep
That like a burning secret which doth go
Even from the bosom that would hoard and
keep;
Emerge thou mayst from the last whelming
sea,
And prove that death but routs life into victory.

Falstaff's Lament Over Prince Hal Become Henry V

One that I cherished,
Yea, loved as a son
Up early, up late with,
My promising one:
No use in good nurture,
None, lads, none!

Here on this settle
He wore the true crown,
King of good fellows,
And Fat Jack was one
Now, Beadle of England
In formal array
Best fellow alive
On a throne flung away!

Companions and cronies
Keep fast and lament;
Come, drawer, more sack here
To drown discontent;
For now intuitions
Shall wither to codes,
Pragmatized morals
Shall libel the gods.

One I instructed,
Yea, talked to -alone:
Precept -example
Clean away thrown!

Sorrow makes thirsty:
Sack, drawer, more sack!
One that I prayed for,
I, Honest Jack!

To bring down these grey hairs -
To cut his old pal!
But, I'll be magnanimous -
Here's to thee Hal!

Greek Architecture

Not magnitude, not lavishness,
But Form—the Site;
Not innovating wilfulness,
But reverence for the Archetype.

Far Off Shore

Look, the raft, a signal flying,
Thin, a shred;
None upon the lashed spars lying,
Quick or dead.

Cries the sea-fowl, hovering over,
'Crew, the crew?'
And the billow, reckless, rover,
Sweeps anew!

Gold In The Mountain

Gold in the mountain,
And gold in the glen,
And greed in the heart,
Heaven having no part,
And unsatisfied men.

Fragments Of A Lost Gnostic Poem Of The Twelfth Century

Found a family, build a state,
The pledged event is still the same:
Matter in end will never abate
His ancient brutal claim.

Indolence is heaven's ally here,
And energy the child of hell:
The Good Man pouring from his pitcher clear
But brims the poisoned well.

From The Conflict Of Convictions

1860-1

The Ancient of Days forever is young,
Forever the scheme of Nature thrives;
I know a wind in purpose strong
It spins against the way it drives.
What if the gulfs their slimed foundations
bare?
So deep must the stones be hurled
Whereon the throes of ages rear
The final empire and the happier world.

Power unanointed may come
Dominion (unsought by the free)
And the Iron Dome,
Stronger for stress and strain,
Fling her huge shadow athwart the main;
But the Founders' dream shall flee.
Age after age has been,
(From man's changeless heart their way they
win);
And death be busy with all who strive
Death, with silent negative.

Yea and Nay
Each hath his say;
But God He keeps the middle way.
None was by
When He spread the sky;
Wisdom is vain, and prophecy.

Gold

We rovers bold,
To the land of Gold,
Over the bowling billows are gliding:
Eager to toil,
For the golden spoil,
And every hardship biding.
See! See!
Before our prows' resistless dashes
The gold-fish fly in golden flashes!
'Neath a sun of gold,
We rovers bold,
On the golden land are gaining;
And every night,
We steer aright,
By golden stars unwaning!
All fires burn a golden glare:
No locks so bright as golden hair!
All orange groves have golden gushings;
All mornings dawn with golden flushings!
In a shower of gold, say fables old,

A maiden was won by the god of gold!
In golden goblets wine is beaming:
On golden couches kings are dreaming!
The Golden Rule dries many tears!
The Golden Number rules the spheres!
Gold, gold it is, that sways the nations:
Gold! gold! the center of all rotations!
On golden axles worlds are turning:
With phosphorescence seas are burning!
All fire-flies flame with golden gleamings!
Gold-hunters' hearts with golden dreamings!
With golden arrows kings are slain:
With gold we'll buy a freeman's name!
In toilsome trades, for scanty earnings,
At home we've slaved, with stifled yearnings:
No light! no hope! Oh, heavy woe!
When nights fled fast, and days dragged slow.
But joyful now, with eager eye,
Fast to the Promised Land we fly:
Where in deep mines,
The treasure shines;
Or down in beds of golden streams,
The gold-flakes glance in golden gleams!
How we long to sift,
That yellow drift!
Rivers! Rivers! cease your goings!
Sand-bars! rise, and stay the tide!
'Till we've gained the golden flowing;
And in the golden haven ride!

Healed Of My Hurt

Healed of my hurt, I laud the inhuman Sea
Yea, bless the Angels Four that there convene;
For healed I am even by the pitiless breath
Distilled in wholesome dew named rosmarine.

Herba Santa

I

After long wars when comes release
Not olive wands proclaiming peace
Can import dearer share
Than stems of Herba Santa hazed
In autumn's Indian air.
Of moods they breathe that care disarm,
They pledge us lenitive and calm.

II

Shall code or creed a lure afford
To win all selves to Love's accord?

When Love ordained a supper divine
For the wide world of man,
What bickerings o'er his gracious wine!
Then strange new feuds began.

Effectual more in lowlier way,
Pacific Herb, thy sensuous plea
The bristling clans of Adam sway
At least to fellowship in thee!
Before thine altar tribal flags are furled,
Fain wouldst thou make one hearthstone of
the world.

III
To scythe, to sceptre, pen and hod
Yea, sodden laborers dumb;
To brains overplied, to feet that plod,
In solace of the Truce of God
The Calumet has come!

IV
Ah for the world ere Raleigh's find
Never that knew this suasive balm
That helps when Gilead's fails to heal,
Helps by an interserted charm.

Insinuous thou that through the nerve
Windest the soul, and so canst win
Some from repinings, some from sin,
The Church's aim thou dost subserve.

The ruffled fag fordone with care
And brooding, God would ease this pain:
Him soothest thou and smoothest down
Till some content return again.

Even ruffians feel thy influence breed
Saint Martin's summer in the mind,
They feel this last evangel plead,
As did the first, apart from creed,
Be peaceful, man, be kind!

V
Rejected once on higher plain,
O Love supreme, to come again
Can this be thine?
Again to come, and win us too
In likeness of a weed
That as a god didst vainly woo,
As man more vainly bleed?

VI
Forbear, my soul! and in thine Eastern
chamber
Rehearse the dream that brings the long
release:
Through jasmine sweet and talismanic amber
Inhaling Herba Santa in the passive Pipe
of Peace.

Immolated

Children of my happier prime,
When One yet lived with me, and threw
Her rainbow over life and time,
Even Hope, my bride, and mother to you!
O, nurtured in sweet pastoral air,
And fed on flowers and light and dew
Of morning meadows -spare, ah, spare
Reproach; spare, and upbraid me not
That, yielding scarce to reckless mood,
But jealous of your future lot,
I sealed you in a fate subdued.
Have I not saved you from the dread
Theft, and ignoring which need be
The triumph of the insincere
Unanimous Mediocrity?
Rest, therefore, free from all despite,
Snugged in the arms of comfortable night.

In The Prison Pen
1864

Listless he eyes the palisades
And sentries in the glare;
'Tis barren as a pelican-beach
But his world is ended there.

Nothing to do; and vacant hands
Bring on the idiot-pain;
He tries to think, to recollect,
But the blur is on his brain.

Around him swarm the plaining ghosts
Like those on Virgil's shore
A wilderness of faces dim,
And pale ones gashed and hoar.

A smiting sun. No shed, no tree;
He totters to his lair
A den that sick hands dug in earth

Ere famine wasted there,

Or, dropping in his place, he swoons,
Walled in by throngs that press,
Till forth from the throngs they bear
him dead
Dead in his meagreness.

Invocation

Ha, ha, gods and kings; fill high, one and all;
Drink, drink! shout and drink! mad respond to
the call!
Fill fast, and fill full; 'gainst the goblet ne'er
sin;
Quaff there, at high tide, to the uttermost
rim:
Flood-tide, and soul-tide to the brim!

Who with wine in him fears? who thinks of his
cares?
Who sighs to be wise, when wine in him flares?
Water sinks down below, in currents full slow;
But wine mounts on high with its genial glow:
Welling up, till the brain overflow!

As the spheres, with a roll, some fiery of soul,
Others golden, with music, revolve round the
pole;
So let our cups, radiant with many hued wines,
Round and round in groups circle, our Zodiac's
Signs:
Round reeling, and ringing their chimes!

Then drink, gods and kings; wine merriment
brings;
It bounds through the veins; there, jubilant
sings.
Let it ebb, then, and flow; wine never grows
dim;
Drain down that bright tide at the foam beaded
rim:
Fill up, every cup, to the brim!

Jack Roy

Kept up by relays of generations young
Never dies at halyards the blithe chorus sung;
While in sands, sounds, and seas where the
storm-petrels cry,

Dropped mute around the globe, these halyard
singers lie.
Short-lived the clippers for racing-cups that
run,
And speeds in life's career many a lavish
mother's-son.

But thou, manly king o' the old Splendid's
crew,
The ribbons o' thy hat still a-fluttering, should
Fly
A challenge, and forever, nor the bravery
should rue.
Only in a tussle for the starry flag high,
When 'tis piety to do, and privilege to die.
Then, only then, would heaven think to lop
Such a cedar as the captain o' the Splendid's
main-top:
A belted sea-gentleman; a gallant, off-hand
Mercutio indifferent in life's gay command.
Magnanimous in humor; when the splintering
shot fell,
'Tooth-picks a-plenty, lads; thank 'em with a
shell!'

Sang Larry o' the Cannakin, smuggler o' the
wine,
At mess between guns, lad in jovial recline:
'In Limbo our Jack he would chirrup up a
cheer,
The martinet there find a chaffing mutineer;
From a thousand fathoms down under hatches
o' your Hades,
He'd ascend in love-ditty, kissing fingers to
your ladies!'

Never relishing the knave, though allowing
for the menial,
Nor overmuch the king, Jack, nor prodigally
genial.
Ashore on liberty he flashed in escapade,
Vaulting over life in its levelness of grade,
Like the dolphin off Africa in rainbow
a-sweeping
Arch iridescent shot from seas languid
sleeping.

Larking with thy life, if a joy but a toy,
Heroic in thy levity wert thou, Jack Roy.

L'Envoi
The Return of the Sire de Nesle.
A.D. 16

My towers at last! These rovings end,
Their thirst is slaked in larger dearth:
The yearning infinite recoils,
For terrible is earth.

Kaf thrusts his snouted crags through fog:
Araxes swells beyond his span,
And knowledge poured by pilgrimage
Overflows the banks of man.

But thou, my stay, thy lasting love
One lonely good, let this but be!
Weary to view the wide world's swarm,
But blest to fold but thee.

Lines Traced Under An Image Of Amor Threatening
Fear me, virgin whosoever
Taking pride from love exempt,
Fear me, slighted. Never, never
Brave me, nor my fury tempt:
Downy wings, but wroth they beat
Tempest even in reason's seat.

Lone Founts
Though fast youth's glorious fable flies,
View not the world with worldling's eyes;
Nor turn with weather of the time.
Foreclose the coming of surprise:
Stand where Posterity shall stand;
Stand where the Ancients stood before,
And, dipping in lone founts thy hand,
Drink of the never-varying lore:
Wise once, and wise thence evermore.

Look-Out Mountain
Who inhabiteth the Mountain
That it shines in lurid light,
And is rolled about with thunders,
And terrors, and a blight,
Like Kaf the peak of Eblis-
Kaf, the evil height?

Who has gone up with a shouting
And a trumpet in the night?

There is battle in the Mountain-
Might assaulteth Might;
'Tis the fastness of the Anarch,
Torrent-torn, an ancient height;
The crags resound the clangor
Of the war of Wrong and Right;
And the armies in the valley
Watch and pray for dawning light.

Joy, joy, the day is breaking,
And the cloud is rolled from sight;
There is triumph in the Morning
For the Anarch's plunging flight;
God has glorified the Mountain
Where a banner burneth bright,
And the armies of the valley
They are fortified in right.

Marlena

Far off in the sea is Marlena,
A land of shades and streams,
A land of many delights,
Dark and bold, thy shores, Marlena;
But green, and timorous, thy soft knolls,
Crouching behind the woodlands.
All shady thy hills; all gleaming thy springs,
Like eyes in the earth looking at you.
How charming thy haunts, Marlena!
Oh, the waters that flow through Onimoo;
Oh, the leaves that rustle through Ponoo:
Oh, the roses that blossom in Tarma.
Come, and see the valley of Vina:
How sweet, how sweet, the Isles from Hina:
'Tis aye afternoon of the full, full moon,
And ever the season of fruit,
And ever the hour of flowers,
And never the time of rains and gales,
All in and about Marlena.
Soft sigh the boughs in the stilly air,
Soft lap the beach the billows there;
And in the woods or by the streams,
You needs must nod in the Land of Dreams.

Misgivings

When ocean-clouds over inland hills
Sweep storming in late autumn brown,

And horror the sodden valley fills,
And the spire falls crashing in the town,
I muse upon my country's ills
The tempest burning from the waste of Time
On the world's fairest hope linked with man's foulest crime.

Nature's dark side is heeded now
(Ah! optimist-cheer dishartened flown)
A child may read the moody brow
Of yon black mountain lone.
With shouts the torrents down the gorges go,
And storms are formed behind the storms we feel:
The hemlock shakes in the rafter, the oak in the driving keel.

Monody

To have known him, to have loved him
After loneness long;
And then to be estranged in life,
And neither in the wrong;
And now for death to set his seal
Ease me, a little ease, my song!

By wintry hills his hermit-mound
The sheeted snow-drifts drape,
And houseless there the snow-bird flits
Beneath the fir-trees' crape:
Glazed now with ice the cloistral vine
That hid the shyest grape.

Off Cape Colonna

Aloof they crown the foreland lone,
From aloft they loftier rise
Fair columns, in the aureole rolled
From sunned Greek seas and skies.
They wax, sublimed to fancy's view,
A god-like group against the blue.

Over much like gods! Serene they saw
The wolf-waves board the deck,
And headlong hull of Falconer,
And many a deadlier wreck.

Old Counsel

Of The Young Master of a Wrecked California Clipper

Come out of the Golden Gate,
Go round the Horn with streamers,

Carry royals early and late;
But, brother, be not over-elate
All hands save ship! has startled dreamers.

Pebbles

I

Though the Clerk of the Weather insist,
And lay down the weather-law,
Pintado and gannet they wist
That the winds blow whither they list
In tempest or flaw.

II

Old are the creeds, but stale the schools,
Revamped as the mode may veer,
But Orm from the schools to the beaches
strays
And, finding a Conch hoar with time, he
delays
And reverent lifts it to ear.
That Voice, pitched in far monotone,
Shall it swerve? shall it deviate ever?
The Seas have inspired it, and Truth
Truth, varying from sameness never.

III

In hollows of the liquid hills
Where the long Blue Ridges run,
The flattery of no echo thrills,
For echo the seas have none;
Nor aught that gives man back man's strain
The hope of his heart, the dream in his brain.

IV

On ocean where the embattled fleets repair,
Man, suffering inflictor, sails on sufferance
there.

V

Implacable I, the old Implacable Sea:
Implacable most when most I smile serene
Pleased, not appeased, by myriad wrecks in
me.

VI

Curled in the comb of yon billow Andean,
Is it the Dragon's heaven-challenging crest?
Elemental mad ramping of ravening waters
Yet Christ on the Mount, and the dove in
her nest!

VII

Healed of my hurt, I laud the inhuman Sea
Yea, bless the Angels Four that there convene;
For healed I am ever by their pitiless breath
Distilled in wholesome dew named rosmarine.

Pipe Song

Care is all stuff:
Puff! Puff!
To puff is enough:
Puff! Puff
More musky than snuff,
And warm is a puff:
Puff! Puff
Here we sit mid our puffs,
Like old lords in their ruffs,
Snug as bears in their muffs:
Puff! Puff
Then puff, puff, puff,
For care is all stuff,
Puffed off in a puff
Puff! Puff!

Shelley's Vision

Wandering late by morning seas
When my heart with pain was low
Hate the censor pelted me
Deject I saw my shadow go.

In elf-caprice of bitter tone
I too would pelt the pelted one:
At my shadow I cast a stone.

When lo, upon that sun-lit ground
I saw the quivering phantom take
The likeness of St. Stephen crowned:
Then did self-reverence awake.

Sheridan At Cedar Creek

(October, 1864)

Shoe the steed with silver
That bore him to the fray,
When he heard the guns at dawning-
Miles away;
When he heard them calling, calling

Mount! nor stay:
Quick, or all is lost;
They've surprised and stormed the post.
They push your routed host
Gallop! retrieve the day.

House the horse in ermine
For the foam-flake blew
White through red October;
He thundered into view;
They cheered him in the looming,
Horseman and horse they knew.
The turn of the tide began,
The rally of bugles ran,
He swung his hat in the van;
The electric hoof-spark flew.

Wreathe the steed and lead him
For the charge he led
Touched and turned the cypress
Into amaranths for the head
Of Philip, king of riders,
Who raised them from the dead
The camp (at dawning lost),
By eve, recovered-forced,
Rang with the laughter of the host
At belated Early fled.

Shroud the horse in sable-
For the mounds they heap!
There is firing in the Valley,
And yet no strife they keep;
It is the parting volley,
It is the pathos deep.
There is glory for the brave
Who lead, and nobly save,
But no knowledge in the grave
Where the nameless followers sleep.

Song Of Yoomy
Departed the pride, and the glory of Mardi:
The vaunt of her isles sleeps deep in the sea,
That rolls o'er his corse with a hush,
His warriors bend over their spears,
His sisters gaze upward and mourn.
Weep, weep, for Adondo is dead!
The sun has gone down in a shower;
Buried in clouds the face of the moon;
Tears stand in the eyes of the starry skies,
And stand in the eyes of the flowers;

And streams of tears are the trickling brooks,
Coursing adown the mountains.
Departed the pride, and the glory of Mardi:
The vaunt of her isles sleeps deep in the sea.
Fast falls the small rain on its bosom that
sobs,
Not showers of rain, but the tears of Oro.

The Aeolian Harp
At The Surf Inn

List the harp in window wailing
Stirred by fitful gales from sea:
Shrieking up in mad crescendo
Dying down in plaintive key!

Listen: less a strain ideal
Than Ariel's rendering of the Real.
What that Real is, let hint
A picture stamped in memory's mint.

Braced well up, with beams aslant,
Betwixt the continents sails the Phocion,
For Baltimore bound from Alicant.
Blue breezy skies white fleeces fleck
Over the chill blue white-capped ocean:
From yard-arm comes 'Wreck ho, a
wreck!'

Dismasted and adrift,
Longtime a thing forsaken;
Overwashed by every wave
Like the slumbering kraken;
Heedless if the billow roar,
Oblivious of the lull,
Leagues and leagues from shoal or shore,
It swims, a levelled hull:
Bulwarks gone, a shaven wreck,
Nameless and a grass-green deck.
A lumberman: perchance, in hold
Prostrate pines with hemlocks rolled.

It has drifted, waterlogged,
Till by trailing weeds beclogged:
Drifted, drifted, day by day,
Pilotless on pathless way.
It has drifted till each plank
Is oozy as the oyster-bank:
Drifted, drifted, night by night,
Craft that never shows a light;

Nor ever, to prevent worse knell,
Tolls in fog the warning bell.

From collision never shrinking,
Drive what may through darksome smother;
Saturate, but never sinking,
Fatal only to the other!
Deadlier than the sunken reef
Since still the snare it shifteth,
Torpid in dumb ambuscade
Waylayingly it drifteth.

O, the sailors, O, the sails!
O, the lost crews never heard of!
Well the harp of Ariel wails
Thought that tongue can tell no word of!

The Age Of The Antoines

While faith forecasts millennial years
Spite Europe's embattled lines,
Back to the Past one glance be cast
The Age of the Antonines!
O summit of fate, O zenith of time
When a pagan gentleman reigned,
And the olive was nailed to the inn of the
world
Nor the peace of the just was feigned.
A halcyon Age, afar it shines,
Solstice of Man and the Antonines.

Hymns to the nations' friendly gods
Went up from the fellowly shrines,
No demagogue beat the pulpit-drum
In the Age of the Antonines!
The sting was not dreamed to be taken from
death,
No Paradise pledged or sought,
But they reasoned of fate at the flowing feast,
Nor stifled the fluent thought,
We sham, we shuffle while faith declines
They were frank in the Age of the Antonines.

Orders and ranks they kept degree,
Few felt how the parvenu pines,
No law-maker took the lawless one's fee
In the Age of the Antonines!
Under law made will the world reposed
And the ruler's right confessed,
For the heavens elected the Emperor then,
The foremost of men the best.

Ah, might we read in America's signs
The Age restored of the Antonines.

The Apparition – A Retrospect

Convulsions came; and, where the field
Long slept in pastoral green,
A goblin-mountain was upheaved
(Sure the scared sense was all deceived),
Marl-glen and slag-ravine.

The unreserve of Ill was there,
The clinkers in her last retreat;
But, ere the eye could take it in,
Or mind could comprehension win,
It sunk! - and at our feet.

So, then, Solidity's a crust
The core of fire below;
All may go well for many a year,
But who can think without a fear
Of horrors that happen so?

The Bench Of Boors

In bed I muse on Tenier's boors,
Embrowned and beery losels all;
A wakeful brain
Elaborates pain:
Within low doors the slugs of boors
Laze and yawn and doze again.

In dreams they doze, the drowsy boors,
Their hazy hovel warm and small:
Thought's ampler bound
But chill is found:
Within low doors the basking boors
Snugly hug the ember-mound.

Sleepless, I see the slumberous boors
Their blurred eyes blink, their eyelids fall:
Thought's eager sight
Aches, overbright!
Within low doors the boozy boors
Cat-naps take in pipe-bowl light.

The Berg (A Dream)

I saw a ship of material build
(Her standards set, her brave apparel on)
Directed as by madness mere

Against a solid iceberg steer,
Nor budge it, though the infactuate ship went down.
The impact made huge ice-cubes fall
Sullen in tons that crashed the deck;
But that one avalanche was all
No other movement save the foundering wreck.

Along the spurs of ridges pale,
Not any slenderest shaft and frail,
A prism over glass-green gorges lone,
Toppled; or lace or traceries fine,
Nor pendant drops in grot or mine
Were jarred, when the stunned ship went down.
Nor sole the gulls in cloud that wheeled
Circling one snow-flanked peak afar,
But nearer fowl the floes that skimmed
And crystal beaches, felt no jar.
No thrill transmitted stirred the lock
Of jack-straw neddle-ice at base;
Towers indermined by waves, the block
Atilt impending, kept their place.
Seals, dozing sleek on sliddery ledges
Slipt never, when by loftier edges
Through the inertia ovrthrown,
The impetuous ship in bafflement went down.

Hard Berg (methought), so cold, so vast,
With mortal damps self-overcast;
Exhaling still thy dankish breath
Adrift dissolving, bound for death;
Though lumpish thou, a lumbering one
A lumbering lubbard loitering slow,
Impingers rue thee ad go slow
Sounding thy precipice below,
Nor stir the slimy slug that sprawls
Along thy dead indifference of walls.

The Enthusiast
"Though He slay me, yet will I trust in Him"

Shall hearts that beat no base retreat
In youth's magnanimous years -
Ignoble hold it, if discreet
When interest tames to fears;
Shall spirits that worship light
Perfidious deem its sacred glow,
Recant, and trudge where worldlings go,
Conform and own them right?

Shall Time with creeping influence cold

Unnerve and cow? The heart
Pine for the heartless ones enrolled
With palterers of the mart?
Shall faith abjure her skies,
Or pale probation blench her down
To shrink from Truth so still, so lone
Mid loud gregarious lies?

Each burning boat in Caesar's rear,
Flames -No return through me!
So put the torch to ties though dear,
If ties but tempters be.
Nor cringe if come the night:
Walk through the cloud to meet the pall,
Though light forsake thee, never fall
From fealty to light.

The Enviable Isles
From 'Rammon.'

Through storms you reach them and from
storms are free.
Afar descried, the foremost drear in hue,
But, nearer, green; and, on the marge, the sea
Makes thunder low and mist of rainbowed
dew.

But, inland, where the sleep that folds the hills
A dreamier sleep, the trance of God, instills
On uplands hazed, in wandering airs
aswoon,
Slow-swaying palms salute love's cypress tree
Adown in vale where pebbly runlets croon
A song to lull all sorrow and all glee.

Sweet-fern and moss in many a glade are here.
Where, strewn in flocks, what cheek-flushed
myriads lie
Dimpling in dream, unconscious slumberers
mere,
While billows endless round the beaches die.

The Figure Head
The Charles-and-Emma seaward sped,
(Named from the carven pair at prow,)
He so smart, and a curly head,
She tricked forth as a bride knows how:
Pretty stem for the port, I trow!

But iron-rust and alum-spray
And chafing gear, and sun and dew
Vexed this lad and lassie gay,
Tears in their eyes, salt tears nor few;
And the hug relaxed with the failing glue.

But came in end a dismal night,
With creaking beams and ribs that groan,
A black lee-shore and waters white:
Dropped on the reef, the pair lie prone:
O, the breakers dance, but the winds they
moan!

The Good Craft Snow Bird

Strenuous need that head-wind be
From purposed voyage that drives at last
The ship, sharp-braced and dogged still,
Beating up against the blast.

Brigs that figs for market gather,
Homeward-bound upon the stretch,
Encounter oft this uglier weather
Yet in end their port they fetch.

Mark yon craft from sunny Smyrna
Glazed with ice in Boston Bay;
Out they toss the fig-drums cheerly,
Livelier for the frosty ray.

What if sleet off-shore assailed her,
What though ice yet plate her yards;
In wintry port not less she renders
Summer's gift with warm regards!

And, look, the underwriters' man,
Timely, when the stevedore's done,
Puts on his specs to pry and scan,
And sets her down A, No. 1.

Bravo, master! Bravo, brig!
For slanting snows out of the West
Never the Snow-Bird cares one fig;
And foul winds steady her, though a pest.

The House-Top

No sleep. The sultriness pervades the air
And blinds the brain-a dense oppression, such
As tawny tigers feel in matted shades,
Vexing their blood and making apt for ravage.

Beneath the stars the roofy desert spreads
Vacant as Libya. All is hushed near by.
Yet fitfully from far breaks a mixed surf
Of muffled sound, the Atheist roar of riot.
Yonder, where parching Sirius set in drought,
Balefully glares red Arson-there-and there.
The town is taken by its rats-ship-rats
And rats of the wharves. All civil charms
And priestly spells which late held hearts in awe
Fear-bound, subjected to a better sway
Than sway of self; these like a dream dissolve
And man rebounds whole aeons back in nature.
Hail to the low dull rumble, dull and dead,
And ponderous drag that jars the wall.
Wise Draco comes, deep in the midnight roll
Of black artillery; he comes, though late;
In code corroborating Calvin's creed
And cynic tyrranies of honest kings;
He comes, nor parlies; and the Town, redeeemed,
Gives thanks devout; nor, being thankful, heeds
The grimy slur on the Republic's faith implied,
Which holds that man is naturally good,
And-more-is Nature's Roman, never to be scourged.

The Land Of Love

Hail! voyagers, hail!
Whence e'er ye come, where'er ye rove,
No calmer strand,
No sweeter land,
Will e'er ye view, than the Land of Love!

Hail! voyagers, hail!
To these, our shores, soft gales invite:
The palm plumes wave,
The billows lave,
And hither point fix'd stars of light!

Hail! voyagers, hail!
Think not our groves wide brood with gloom;
In this, our isle,
Bright flowers smile:
Full urns, rose-heaped, these valleys bloom.

Hail! voyagers, hail!
Be not deceived; renounce vain things;
Ye may not find
A tranquil mind,
Though hence ye sail with swiftest wings.

Hail! voyagers, hail!

Time flies full fast; life soon is o'er;
And ye may mourn,
That hither borne,
Ye left behind our pleasant shore.

The Maldive Shark

About the Shark, phlegmatical one,
Pale sot of the Maldive sea,
The sleek little pilot-fish, azure and slim,
How alert in attendance be.
From his saw-pit of mouth, from his charnel of maw,
They have nothing of harm to dread,
But liquidly glide on his ghastly flank
Or before his Gorgonian head;
Or lurk in the port of serrated teeth
In white triple tiers of glittering gates,
And there find a haven when peril's abroad,
An asylum in jaws of the Fates!
They are friends; and friendly they guide him to prey,
Yet never partake of the treat
Eyes and brains to the dotard lethargic and dull,
Pale ravener of horrible meat.

The Marchioness Of Brinvilliers

He toned the sprightly beam of morning
With twilight meek of tender eve,
Brightness interfused with softness,
Light and shade did weave:
And gave to candor equal place
With mystery starred in open skies;
And, floating all in sweetness, made
Her fathomless mild eyes.

The Mound By The Lake

The grass shall never forget this grave.
When homeward footing it in the sun
After the weary ride by rail,
The stripling soldiers passed her door,
Wounded perchance, or wan and pale,
She left her household work undone
Duly the wayside table spread,
With evergreens shaded, to regale
Each travel-spent and grateful one.
So warm her heart, childless, unwed,
Who like a mother comforted.

The New Zealot To The Sun

Persian, you rise
Aflame from climes of sacrifice
Where adulators sue,
And prostrate man, with brow abased,
Adheres to rites whose tenor traced
All worship hitherto.

Arch type of sway,
Meetly your over-ruling ray
You fling from Asia's plain,
Whence flashed the javelins abroad
Of many a wild incursive horde
Led by some shepherd Cain.

Mid terrors dinned
Gods too came conquerors from your Ind,
The book of Brahma throve;
They came like to the scythed car,
Westward they rolled their empire far,
Of night their purple wove.

Chemist, you breed
In orient climes each sorcerous weed
That energizes dream
Transmitted, spread in myths and creeds,
Houris and hells, delirious screeds
And Calvin's last extreme.

What though your light
In time's first dawn compelled the flight
Of Chaos' startled clan,
Shall never all your darted spears
Disperse worse Anarchs, frauds and fears,
Sprung from these weeds to man?

But Science yet
An effluence ampler shall beget,
And power beyond your play
Shall quell the shades you fail to rout,
Yea, searching every secret out
Elucidate your ray.

The Portent

Hanging from the beam,
Slowly swaying (such the law),
Gaunt the shadow on the green,
Shenandoah!
The cut is on the crown
(Lo, John Brown),

And the stabs shall heal no more.

Hidden in the cap
Is the anguish none can draw;
So your future veils its face,
Shenandoah!
But the streaming beard is shown
(Weird John Brown),
The meteor of the war.

The Ravaged Villa

In shards the sylvan vases lie,
Their links of dance undone,
And brambles wither by thy brim,
Choked fountain of the sun!
The spider in the laurel spins,
The weed exiles the flower:
And, flung to kiln, Apollo's bust
Makes lime for Mammon's tower.

The Stone Fleet

I have a feeling for those ships,
Each worn and ancient one,
With great bluff bows, and broad in the beam:
Ay, it was unkindly done.
But so they serve the Obsolete
Even so, Stone Fleet!

You'll say I'm doting; do but think
I scudded round the Horn in one
The Tenedos, a glorious
Good old craft as ever run
Sunk (how all unmeet!)
With the Old Stone Fleet.

An India ship of fame was she,
Spices and shawls and fans she bore;
A whaler when her wrinkles came
Turned off! till, spent and poor,
Her bones were sold (escheat)!
Ah! Stone Fleet.

Four were erst patrician keels
(Names attest what families be),
The Kensington, and Richmond too,
Leonidas and Lee:
But now they have their seat
With the Old Stone Fleet.

To scuttle them-a pirate deed
Sack them, and dismast;
They sunk so slow, they died so hard,
But gurgling dropped at last.
Their ghosts in gales repeat
Woe's us, Stone Fleet!

And all for naught. The waters pass
Currents will have their way;
Nature is nobody's ally; 'tis well;
The harbor is bettered-will stay.
A failure, and complete,
Was your Old Stone Fleet.

The Swamp Angel

There is a coal-black Angel
With a thick Afric lip,
And he dwells (like the hunted and harried)
In a swamp where the green frogs dip.
But his face is against a City
Which is over a bay of the sea,
And he breathes with a breath that is
blastment,
And dooms by a far decree.

By night there is fear in the City,
Through the darkness a star soareth on;
There's a scream that screams up to the zenith,
Then the poise of a meteor lone
Lighting far the pale fright of the faces,
And downward the coming is seen;
Then the rush, and the burst, and the havoc,
And wails and shrieks between.

It comes like the thief in the gloaming;
It comes, and none may foretell
The place of the coming, the glaring;
They live in a sleepless spell
That wizens, and withers, and whitens;
It ages the young, and the bloom
Of the maiden is ashes of roses
The Swamp Angel broods in his gloom.

Swift is his messengers' going,
But slowly he saps their halls,
As if by delay deluding.
They move from their crumbling walls
Farther and farther away;
But the Angel sends after and after,
By night with the flame of his ray

By night with the voice of his screaming
Sends after them, stone by stone,
And farther walls fall, farther portals,
And weed follows weed through the Town.

Is this the proud City? the scorner
Which never would yield the ground?
Which mocked at the coal-black Angel?
The cup of despair goes round.
Vainly he calls upon Michael
(The white man's seraph was he,)
For Michael has fled from his tower
To the Angel over the sea.
Who weeps for the woeful City
Let him weep for our guilty kind;
Who joys at her wild despairing
Christ, the Forgiver, convert his mind.

The Tuft Of Kelp

All dripping in tangles green,
Cast up by a lonely sea
If purer for that, O Weed,
Bitterer, too, are ye?

The Temeraire

The gloomy hulls in armor grim,
Like clouds o'er moors have met,
And prove that oak, and iron, and man
Are tough in fibre yet.

But Splendors wane. The sea-fight yields
No front of old display;
The garniture, emblazonment,
And heraldry all decay.

Towering afar in parting light,
The fleets like Albion's forelands shine
The full-sailed fleets, the shrouded show
Of Ships-of-the-Line.

The fighting Temeraire,
Built of a thousand trees,
Lunging out her lightnings,
And beetling o'er the seas
O Ship, how brave and fair,
That fought so oft and well,

On open decks you manned the gun
Armorial.

What cheerings did you share,
Impulsive in the van,
When down upon leagued France and
Spain
We English ran
The freshet at your bowsprit
Like the foam upon the can.
Bickering, your colors
Licked up the Spanish air,
You flapped with flames of battle-flags
Your challenge, Temeraire!
The rear ones of our fleet
They yearned to share your place,
Still vying with the Victory
Throughout that earnest race
The Victory, whose Admiral,
With orders nobly won,
Shone in the globe of the battle glow
The angel in that sun.
Parallel in story,
Lo, the stately pair,
As late in grapple ranging,
The foe between them there
When four great hulls lay tiered,
And the fiery tempest cleared,
And your prizes twain appeared,
Temeraire!

But Trafalgar is over now,
The quarter-deck undone;
The carved and castled navies fire
Their evening-gun.
O, Titan Temeraire,
Your stern-lights fade away;
Your bulwarks to the years must yield,
And heart-of-oak decay.
A pigmy steam-tug tows you,
Gigantic, to the shore
Dismantled of your guns and spars,
And sweeping wings of war.
The rivets clinch the iron clads,
Men learn a deadlier lore;
But Fame has nailed your battle-flags
Your ghost it sails before:
O, the navies old and oaken,
O, the Temeraire no more!

We Fish

We fish, we fish, we merrily swim,
We care not for friend nor for foe.

Our fins are stout,
Our tails are out,
As through the seas we go.

Fish, Fish, we are fish with red gills;
Naught disturbs us, our blood is at zero:
We are buoyant because of our bags,
Being many, each fish is a hero.
We care not what is it, this life
That we follow, this phantom unknown;
To swim, it's exceedingly pleasant,
So swim away, making a foam.
This strange looking thing by our side,
Not for safety, around it we flee:
Its shadow's so shady, that's all,
We only swim under its lee.
And as for the eels there above,
And as for the fowls of the air,
We care not for them nor their ways,
As we cheerily glide afar!

We fish, we fish, we merrily swim,
We care not for friend nor for foe:
Our fins are stout,
Our tails are out,
As through the seas we go.

To Ned

Where is the world we roved, Ned Bunn?
Hollows thereof lay rich in shade
By voyagers old inviolate thrown
Ere Paul Pry cruised with Pelf and Trade.
To us old lads some thoughts come home
Who roamed a world young lads no more shall
roam.

Nor less the satiate year impends
When, wearying of routine-resorts,
The pleasure-hunter shall break loose,
Ned, for our Pantheistic ports:
Marquesas and glenned isles that be
Authentic Edens in a Pagan sea.

The charm of scenes untried shall lure,
And, Ned, a legend urge the flight
The Typee-truants under stars
Unknown to Shakespere's Midsummer
Night;
And man, if lost to Saturn's Age,
Yet feeling life no Syrian pilgrimage.

But, tell, shall he, the tourist, find
Our isles the same in violet-glow
Enamoring us what years and years
Ah, Ned, what years and years ago!
Well, Adam advances, smart in pace,
But scarce by violets that advance you trace.

But we, in anchor-watches calm,
The Indian Psyche's languor won,
And, musing, breathed primeval balm
From Edens ere yet overrun;
Marvelling mild if mortal twice,
Here and hereafter, touch a Paradise.

To The Master Of The Meteor

Lonesome on earth's loneliest deep,
Sailor! who dost thy vigil keep
Off the Cape of Storms dost musing sweep
Over monstrous waves that curl and comb;
Of thee we think when here from brink
We blow the mead in bubbling foam.

Of thee we think, in a ring we link;
To the shearer of ocean's fleece we drink,
And the Meteor rolling home.

Tom Deadlight

Farewell and adieu to you noble hearties,
Farewell and adieu to you ladies of Spain,
For I've received orders for to sail for the
Deadman,
But hope with the grand fleet to see you
again.

I have hove my ship to, with main-top-sail
aback, boys;
I have hove my ship to, for the strike
soundings clear
The black scud a'flying; but, by God's blessing,
dam' me,
Right up the Channel for the Deadman I'll
steer.

I have worried through the waters that are
called the Doldrums,
And growled at Sargasso that clogs while ye
grope
Blast my eyes, but the light-ship is hid by the

mist, lads:
Flying Dutchman, odds bobs, off the
Cape of Good Hope!

But what's this I feel that is fanning my cheek,
Matt?
The white goney's wing? how she rolls!
't is the Cape!
Give my kit to the mess, Jock, for kin none is
mine, none;
And tell Holy Joe to avast with the crape.

Dead reckoning, says Joe, it won't do to go by;
But they doused all the glims, Matt, in sky
t' other night.
Dead reckoning is good for to sail for the
Deadman;
And Tom Deadlight he thinks it may reckon
near right.

The signal! it streams for the grand fleet to
anchor.
The captains, the trumpets, the hullabaloo!
Stand by for blue-blazes, and mind your
shank-painters,
For the Lord High Admiral, he's squinting
at you!

But give me my tot, Matt, before I roll over;
Jock, let's have your flipper, it's good for to
feel;
And don't sew me up without baccy in mouth,
boys,
And don't blubber like lubbers when I turn
up my keel.

www.ingramcontent.com/pod-product-compliance
Lightning Source LLC
Chambersburg PA
CBHW071745020426
42331CB00008B/2183